A BOOK OF CATS

A BOOK OF CATS

Twenty drawings by Foujita

with

Poems in prose by Michael Joseph

Ashford Press Publishing
Southampton
1987

This edition published by Ashford Press Publishing
1 Church Road
Shedfield
Hampshire SO3 2HW

First published by Covici Friede, New York, 1930

British Library Cataloguing in Publication Data

Foujita, Tsugouharu
    A book of cats. ——— 2nd ed.
    1. Cats in art 2. Drawing, French
    I. Title II. Joseph, Michael, 1897-1958
    741.944   NC783.8.C3
    ISBN 1-85253-036-7

PREFACE

Michael Joseph, (1897-1958) apart from being well-known as an author, a literary agent and a successful publisher, was also a famous devotee of the feline species. He was surrounded by cats most of his life and perhaps the most famous was Charles O'Malley about whom the book Charles – *The Story of a Friendship* was written. He wrote several books about cats, many short stories and articles, and also made radio broadcasts about them.

It is interesting to note that even in the 1930s he was a keen lobbyist for cats to be afforded the same legal protection as that enjoyed by dogs - a matter which cat lovers continue to lobby for to this day. He founded a club for this very purpose, known as the *Companionship of Cat Lovers* and its slogan was 'Justice and better publicity for the Cat'. Amongst the founder members of that club were Compton Mackenzie, Edith Sitwell and Algernon Blackwood.

Michael Joseph was also the first life President of *The Siamese Cat Society of the British Empire* – an organisation that continues to exist and flourish.

Richard Joseph recalls in his biography of his father *(Michael Joseph, Master of Words, Ashford Press Publishing 1986)* that his father was:

'... the epitome of a cat lover or ailurophile ... Michael would argue that only ailurophiles can understand the subtlety of the cat's character. One cannot judge the cat's intelligence fairly by carrying out tests in a laboratory, for it is almost impossible to teach a cat the rudimentary tricks that other animals learn. Cats are temperamentally very unsuited to training and because they are often unwilling to be trained to obey, does not mean that they are unintelligent. Your cat may follow you around and play games with you, but try to exact obedience and you will fail.'

Although *Charles: The Story of a Friendship* sold some 50,000 copies in its first six years, and stirred the emotions of cat lovers everywhere, *A Book of Cats* was only ever published as a limited edition of 500 copies in 1930. It is surprising that Michael Joseph never decided to make it more widely available, since the book is a rare combination of his quite exquisite poetry and the gentle drawings of an internationally renowned artist – Foujita. The poems in prose included in *A Book of Cats* are a sensual exposition of the multifaceted character of the cat and never fail to evoke a true image of this fascinating creature.

They reveal the true understanding of cats which Michael Joseph once outlined in another book of cats, *Cats Company:*

'To win and hold a cat's affection a process of never-ending courtship is necessary. Cats, like women, will not be taken for granted. They must be admired, petted, coaxed into good humour, played with when they are playful, left to themselves when, as often happens, they prefer to be alone. Nothing is more destructive of friendship than attempts to force a cat into something contrary to his mood.'

It is not known how Michael Jospeh came to work with Foujita on the book, since it would have been several years at least before he acquired Charles and prior to his membership of a number of cat clubs. One can only surmise. However, the result was a perfect combination.

Leonard Foujita (1886-1968) was born in Tokyo as Fujita Tsuguji. After graduating from the Department of Western Art at Tokyo School of Fine Arts he went to France in 1913 and soon became friends with and worked under the tutelage of other young artists there, including Soutine, Picasso, Chagall and Modigliani.

His early paintings were of ordinary life in the outskirts of Paris but by about the beginning of the 1920s he had begun to evolve his own distinctive style and was very much admired. He worked in lines drawn with a Japanese make-up brush and specialised in nudes, self-portraits – often with a cat in the background – and room interiors. He became one of the few Japanese painters working in a Western manner to have an international reputation, creating an art that combined Western modernism with Japanese tradition.

Jane F. Tatam
Salisbury
1987

MYRRHA

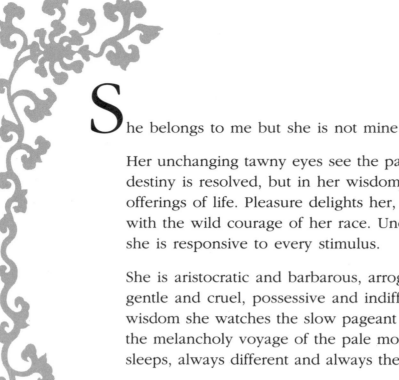

She belongs to me but she is not mine

Her unchanging tawny eyes see the past and the future. Her destiny is resolved, but in her wisdom she takes the offerings of life. Pleasure delights her, danger she will resist with the wild courage of her race. Under her proud mask she is responsive to every stimulus.

She is aristocratic and barbarous, arrogant and supplicating, gentle and cruel, possessive and indifferent. With infinite wisdom she watches the slow pageant of the golden sun and the melancholy voyage of the pale moon. She wakes and sleeps, always different and always the same.

In repose she is vigilant, her claws pleasurably relaxed, her fur-surfaced limbs poised gracefully between lassitude and swift movement. The grace of the lithe young body cloaks her strength.

She can move languorously and with devastating swiftness. The falling rose petal is not gentler than her fond caress, but the swift blow which secures her prey is a scourge.

A fluttering leaf tempts her but she cannot be enticed to play save at her own will. Food cannot secure her submission nor captivity subdue her proud spirit. She has no Master. She is mine but she does not belong to me.

Untamed and untameable, she belongs to the virgin jungle. Civilization has not softened her. Luxury has made her indolent, capricious, selfish; it does not absorb her, she has known it too long. The Pharaohs were her slaves and her heritage of freedom remains untouched.

Strange, beautiful Myrrha! You belong to me but you are not mine.

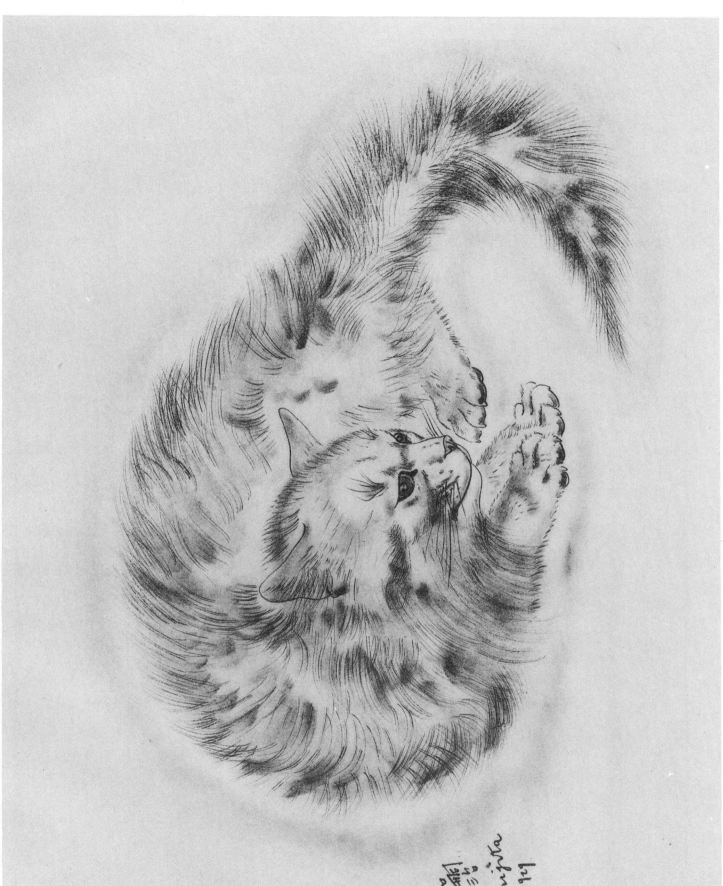

CHRYSOTHEMIS

You have lived before, Chrysothemis, and so have I. This is not the first time we have known each other. Do you remember?

How many centuries of time have passed since last I looked into your eyes? But I remember well. Yet do I remember who I was then, nor you. That veil I cannot lift.

Sometimes I think you know, Chrysothemis. Your eyes recall the past, you cannot speak. But I who can, do not remember. So our communion is silent.

Were you my slave? Was I your master? Perchance you were my royal mistress and I the lowly courtier who loved you.

Now, when you press your sweet-scented fur against my hand, veiling your eyes in fond expression, happily I know our love endures. You sing to me like far-off rolling drums, your velvet gauntlets stretch contentedly, your silken banner waves in graceful token of your case.

No greater love do I desire than this, Chrysothemis, my friend and love. You shall lie by my side, your gently quivering body curled in the hollow of my arm. Then, if you will, stretch wantonly; as long ago, perchance, we shared a couch in Babylon together. I will bury my face in your caressing fur and dream.

We have lived before, Chrysothemis, and shall live again. But this is the hour of our eternal love, when gracious destiny decrees our knowledge of each other. Sleep now, Chrysothemis, and I will guard your slumber. Who knows how long before again we share this mood of rest, content and love.

AHOLIBAH

She is a fickle creature, this Aholibah. There she lies, warming her furred body in the sun, heedless of my beckoning, indifferent to my voice. Maliciously she turns her pretty head away.

Ungrateful wanton! Here I have prepared your bowl of milk, your dish of meat. They do not stir your appetite, it seems; but well I know you will descend, with lazy stretching of your limbs, and lick the platters clean when I am gone.

She mocks me as I linger, calling. Her tail jerks to and fro in mild contempt; she contemplates the smoothness of her rounded paw. She yawns, a graceful insult; prepares herself for sleep.

O hypocrite Aholibah! Patience masters hunger, vanity conceals them both. Why should I stand beseechingly before you, now that I know your mood?

Vain, idle trollop; debauched pagan, incestuous and bold! Away to your companions of the night with their wild cries and lustful joys. Leave me in peace.

The dog, good faithful peasant, shall be my friend. You, perverse aristocrat, shall thus be humbled. Your head turns slowly on your outstretched paws, as if you slept indeed, but I am not deceived. Sleep on and hear my words. I have done with proud Aholibah. My hearth is hers no more; my gates are locked against her entry.

See, I go. Farewell, Aholibah! You wake? Then – here, my sweet one, is the tasty dish; the milk is warm from the cow. Drink sweetly and refresh your weary throat. Aholibah, I love you – why?

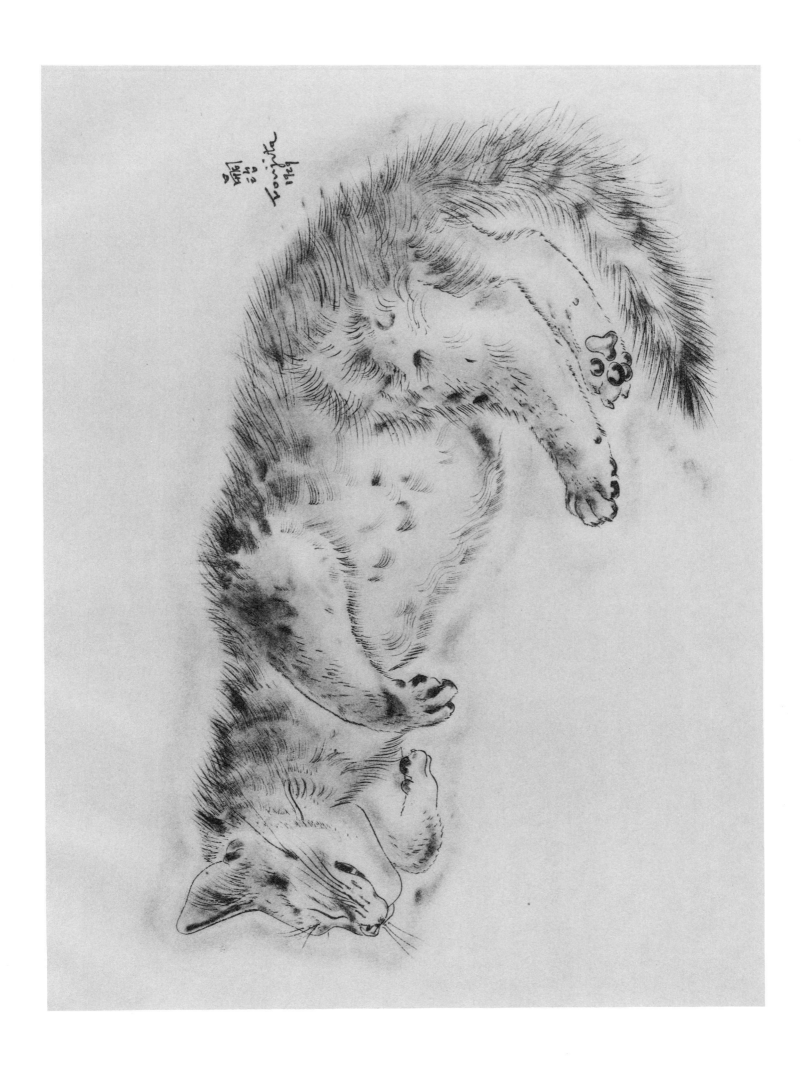

SAPPHO

The timid field mouse is her prey, and the unseeing new-born mole. Yet she will challenge the screaming gull with mighty wing and searing beak; and the dog with slavering jaw and raucous bark will presently retreat before the menace of her unsheathed claws.

The sharp-toothed rat fears Sappho and cannot match her strength and fury. Let the darting fish beware of rising to the surface when Sappho crouches by the water's edge. The lunge of her curved talons will destroy him in that moment.

The venomous serpent is her age-long prey. Sappho alone does not recoil before the flickering poison fangs but swiftly pricks the vulnerable spot of the evil one.

Man cannot tame the proud spirit of Sappho nor compel her to his service. She will accept the offering of food and shelter but yields no more than man deserves. She must be free to go on her occasions. Nothing can daunt her; always will her liberty be cherished above all. Sappho needs no protector, she is the fearless one.

But the night changes her. Now she is afraid, of the things she knows not and cannot see; yet they are phantoms familiar to her eyes.

Under the black robe of the night, she waits, the trembling victim who is never claimed. What dreadful shapes surround her, what terror do they breathe into her lowered ear that she should crouch on quivering limbs, impatient for the dawn?

PASIPHAE

Sleep, coquette, your blandishments avail no more. Now I am delivered of your tyranny awhile.

You do not love me. When, furred siren, you tempt me from my work it is to gratify your vanity. Cajole me as you will, I am familiar with your flattery.

Yet you succeed. How should I write when you disturb my papers? How well you love to thrust a gossamer paw beneath the sheet on which I write and gently disengage it from my hand. Think you that baby mice lurk underneath the surface scratched by my industrious pen?

The sheet is spoiled and so I make a paper ball and throw it for your capture. You seize it fiercely and begin the ancient sport of toying with your prey. But if I work anew you spring upon my knee, proclaiming mischievous intent.

You know I would ignore you; capriciously you coax from me expressions of my love. Your soul delights in praise and adoration. Now upon my knee you play a part, you feign affection to excite my love.

Then you will perambulate my desk, with mincing step avoiding my possessions. Will you not betake yourself elsewhere? You smile at my exasperation; compose yourself for rest and stretch your limbs complacently at length.

Your saffron eyes compel my love but mock my pleading. You will not suffer me to touch your bronze-flecked fur which I admire. Why then torment me?

But now I am released from bondage. Sleep on, coquette Pasiphae. In peace I work, but 't is of you I write.

AZUBAH

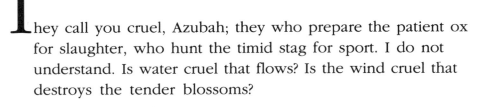

They call you cruel, Azubah; they who prepare the patient ox for slaughter, who hunt the timid stag for sport. I do not understand. Is water cruel that flows? Is the wind cruel that destroys the tender blossoms?

They say you torture wantonly, they who teach the dog to rend the panting fox. They do not understand you must, or lose your heritage of freedom. The practice of your deadly art must be maintained or you in turn will perish with your race. This they do not understand.

I tell you why you are condemned. You hunt, but not for us. The prey is yours. You flay your victim for your pleasure's sake not ours. We, who permit the goring bull to lacerate the already wounded horse, who pierce the lark's eye that he shall sing in bars for our delight, are not amused that you, Azubah, should dare to violate our humane laws.

Our humane laws! What mockery are they, when men destroy their fellows with bullet, bomb and poison gas. Humanity has yet to learn protection from itself.

O wise Azubah, heed not the foolish condemnation of the mob of men. Regard their judgment with an indifferent eye; pursue your prey at will. If it will be cruelty to preserve your kind, be generously cruel.

All that I ask is your return to me when the chase tires you. Come, then, and rest, for no reproach from me shall greet your coming. Here is one who understands.

SEMIRAMIS

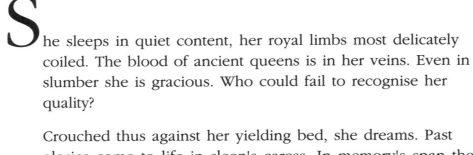

S he sleeps in quiet content, her royal limbs most delicately coiled. The blood of ancient queens is in her veins. Even in slumber she is gracious. Who could fail to recognise her quality?

Crouched thus against her yielding bed, she dreams. Past glories come to life in sleep's caress. In memory's span the Nile flows by her temple walls, the willing slaves surround her with their gifts, she reigns as befits her queenly state.

Now, alas, the temple walls are fallen, the worshippers are gone. But the ancient Nile flows on and Semiramis is sleeping.

She honours me, Semiramis, with her royal company. I must not disturb her slumber nor yield to my desire to touch her if she wills it not. To profane her coat with vulgar hand were insult to her majesty.

She sleeps in quiet content and ponders the splendid past. The green-garlanded altars are now dust before the wind, the wise sorcerers who sought her royal aid have perished with their secrets. But Semiramis lives through all the centuries of time, and sleeps.

Now she rests by my hearth and I rejoice. My humble dwelling is her refuge. Semiramis, I serve you with a glad heart. The caress of your velvet paw when you awake is all the reward I crave.

ATARAH AND HESIONE

Tired out with play, they sleep. In fond embrace they dream their carnival anew.

The hours are passed in happy revelry. They strut and leap, attack, defend, run this way, that way, skirmishing, with blend of darting paw and flashing teeth. Heroic onslaughts meet with fierce resistance; the whirling, struggling bodies lock in rivalry of strength.

A scrap of paper dancing in the wind has tested all their skill. The swift Hesione outruns the spinning prey; Atarah waits and pounces but in vain. No matter, there are other games to play.

Atarah flaunts a challenging tail; Hesione launches furious attack. The kindly earth receives them as they roll, over and over, fighting lustily; Hesione strikes swiftly past Atarah's fending thrusts. Dishevelled but unweary they arise, and forthwith come to grips again.

The unhurried gait, the sidelong prance, the frenzied lashing paws, toy weapons fiercely brandished, all weave the pattern of their future skill.

The chase allures them, be it buzzing fly or moving shadows in the sun. They hurl themselves in vain at yielding grass which flutters in the breeze. So stealthily they creep towards their mark!

Enchanting warrior-babes! The game they play is prelude to reality. Soon they will test their swiftness and their strength in sterner fields. The ordeal is not yet, and they may rest awhile and be refreshed for play.

The armistice of sleep has claimed them now. Companions in their rest as in their sport, they lie and share their dreams.

HARHAS

The noonday sun looks down and still you sleep, Harhas. Your limbs are coiled in ecstasy of weariness. Your platter is untouched since you returned at dawn. Forgetfulness, it seems, is all you seek.

Shameless one, deserting me at beckoning of the moon to wander through the fields. On velvet tread, obeying esoteric rites, you disappeared into the night.

Your eyes shone brightly, for the moon was at the full. Gone was your languor of the day. What meant your silent haste? What strange urgency bade you attend?

Chatte dans le jour

La nuit elle est femme.

Were you so fearful of your changing shape when by my side? Was this the reason of your haste?

Perchance your ruthless errand sent you broomstick-wise across the face of the moon? What arcane rites have you observed? What sorcerer's secrets are you privy to?

You are obedient to the moon but not to me. Mysterious Harhas, must you keep faith with those who summon you imperiously by night? But while I grieve, you sleep, indifferent to my troubled thoughts.

For I am but a mortal and I do not know the portents which direct your steps. Submissive daughter of the moon, sleep on in peace. Your feline grace is all my eyes behold; you owe allegiance to the invisible shapes of beldams, wizards and their craft. The moon, their mistress, moves and you must go.

The noonday sun looks down and still you sleep.

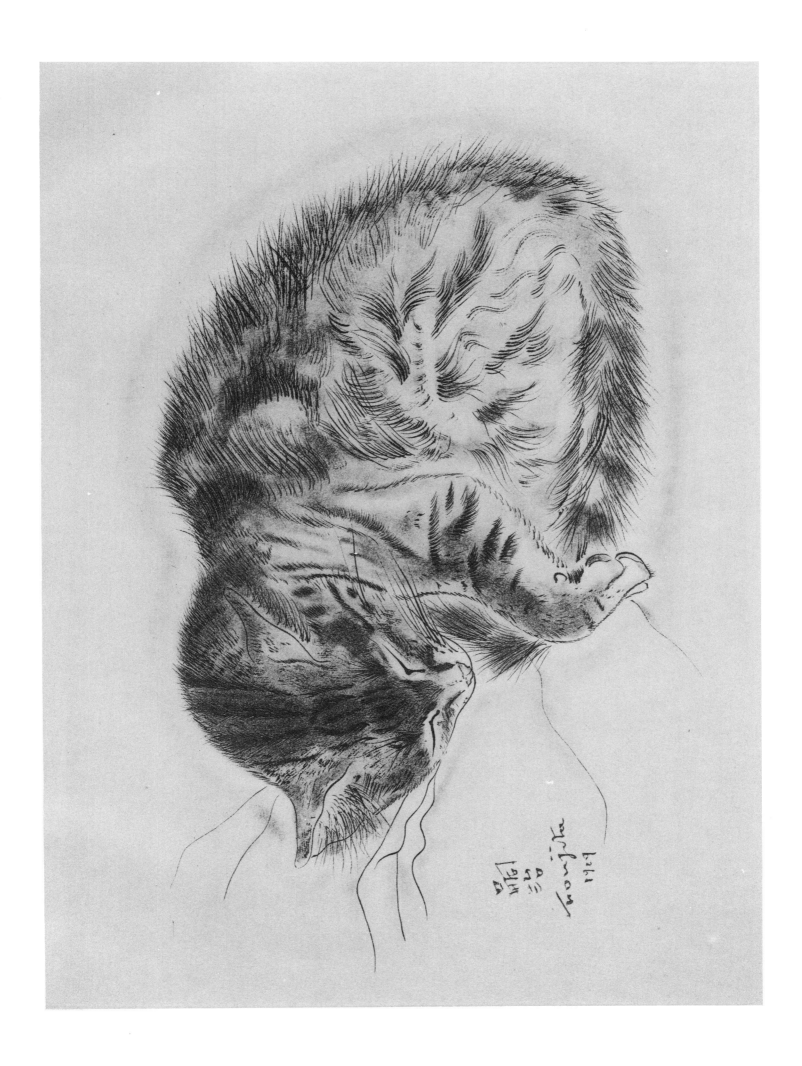

CLEOPATRA

I have had many friends but none so true as Cleopatra. For she will leave me if I please her not. She will not pander to my mood. Forbearance of a friend for friendship's sake is not her creed; and I am glad, for thus I know the truth.

My vanity is curbed by her engaging candour. My harmonies are discord in her ears and her protesting paw will silence them. I am ungentle with her sacred fur and she will turn aside. Her dignified reproach is eloquent.

Pensively she sits alone, indifferent to my call. I understand and am not grieved. It is sincerity which binds her and her aloofness now makes sweeter the caress which presently I may receive.

The boisterous dog dissembles his dislikes and is insensitively made. Not so my Cleopatra. She proclaims an independent spirit in her gait. She lifts her lovely, arrogant head and strolls away; her plume-like tail moves slowly as she goes, in token of her mild displeasure.

If I am angered by her seeming waywardness the fault is mine. The crudity of hand and voice offends her royal person. When I approach her or would speak with her I must observe the niceties of custom.

Patrician Cleopatra! Yet she will unbend and gambol at my feet, or leap upon my knee. My hand may then caress her with rough tenderness. Because I please her she will stay with me.

I have had many friends but none so true as Cleopatra

ABIHAIL

At dawn she leaves my house to roam the fields, lifting her dainty feet through the wet grass. The field-mice scurry away at her approach for they have learned to fear her silent champing jaws. When the sun's rays have dried the earth she will lie outstretched in the tangled undergrowth, in her green eyes a lust of the bright plumage flashing in the sun.

The bird soars into the blue canopy of the sky but Abihail waits patiently, her belly pressed to the warm earth. At last the bird's flight is done; and, quivering, Abihail makes her deadly spring.

Is this my gentle Abihail? The soft insinuation of her velvet paws, the muted music of her voice, the graceful friction of her comely head, all these and other tenderness I know, but the marauding tiger of the fields, can this be Abihail?

Which is the mask and which the true? Is her dear fondness but a slayer's cloak? Does some grim sorcerer seize her in his grip and send her to appease the lust for blood?

Now you are with me I am not afraid; your playful innocence is proof against my fancy. But when you draw aloof and mystically gaze into those things I see not, again I fear the dreadful change. Tell me, O Abihail, what is the message?

Blandly you smile at me, Abihail, and I shall never know. Your green eyes hold their secret.

EPRATH

Now you are appeased, Eprath; the milk you crave is set before you and I will watch you drink.

Your trembling body gratefully receives its due; your wispy tail outstretched in satisfaction and your straddled paws positioned for the feast. The pink tongue flickers to and fro and soon the soft warm belly will be swollen with milk.

Then, satisfied, you will attend your toilet. Diligently the pink tongue will scrape the fur clean and smooth. No milky pearls shall mar your beauty; Eprath has no need of jewels. With moistened paw you will compose the ruffled fur till not a spot remains.

And then an elegant yawn, a drowsy purr; luxurious stretching of your dainty limbs. For sleep invites you after appetite is stilled. Turn round, and round again; observe formality most scrupulously. Prepare to sleep in comfort, and withdraw your paws beneath your body's sheltering warmth.

The eyes blink lazily, as who should say, Now I will rest, with your protection. You need not fear, Eprath, for you are safe with me. Sleep easily and long, renew your strength.

When you awake, refreshed, if you should wander to the empty bowl, lo! you shall find it filled to the brim. I am your patron and thus I hope to win your love.

Sing me a grace, for I provide the sustenance you love; I am rewarded with your tinkling song. Then drink, my Eprath, till the bowl be clean.

AHINOAM

Ahinoam is the turbulent one, mischief incarnate. In those tiny velvet gauntlets lurk sharp and mobile claws which she delights to thrust at me in gentle play.

The shell-pink hollow of her baby mouth will open to reveal the dainty menace of her teeth. In fierce assault she grips my hand and plays the tiger with my yielding flesh.

In sport she lures me on, now huntress, now the hunted. Gracefully she swerves aside and tempts pursuit. Then stealthily she stalks the human foe, in mock solemnity, laughter dancing in her lustrous eyes.

Are you not tired of play, Ahinoam? So tranquilly you contemplate the ground, assuming adult wisdom and repose, that I might be deceived. But mischief hides behind the stately pose and as I move your body quivers with repressed delight. You will elude me with a cunning spring; then, lying on your back, you will defend yourself with lunging limb and darting claw.

How swiftly you will seize my hand between your teeth as I envelop you in smothering grasp; how valiantly you will resist my strength! Your flickering tail – absurd Ahinoam! – betrays your eagerness to play again.

Your challenge is accepted, so beware. I will give chase and with rough gentleness imprison you. Be nimble, Ahinoam, escape me if you can. Your eyes look solemnly away but you are well aware of my design. Now, we shall frolic to your heart's content.

AHOLAH

Content Aholah, now you have your life's desire. Far sweeter this than stalking the elusive prey, more rapturous than the surging passions of the night. The little one, with groping paw and eager mouth, fulfils your destiny and you rejoice.

His plaintive cry is music in your ears and lavishly you answer it. The kneading pressure of the baby claws is exquisite delight and you are prodigal with love.

You sing your throbbing lullaby, inviting rest. The tiny form relaxes into sleep and now your song vibrates triumphantly. I, Aholah, am a mother. So you sing.

How sweet is realized ambition! Now you can lie abandoned to your ease, your travail past and comfort in its stead. Dream of the heritage you will bequeath, the grace and prowess of your race. Surely he will be beautiful and strong.

Soon, when the beloved stirs from your embrace, you will begin the willing task. Imprison him between your paws and let your roughened tongue sweep clean the mottled fur. The god of cleanliness must be obeyed and he must learn the lesson.

Then presently, your waving tail will tempt the babe to play. Thus will the tender limbs acquire their strength and thus swift cunning be implanted for his safety. In fierce mock combat you will teach the arts of hunting and of war. The gentle ruses of maternal love shall gird him for the fray.

Fond, zealous mother, so you have your life's desire. Cherish the little one and sing, I, Aholah, am a mother now.

AMESTRIS

Why should I love her? When I call to her she turns away. She is perverse, secretive, vain. She is primitive and cruel. She is vagabond and thief.

Her cleanliness is not a virtue. When I watch her fastidiously cleaning her velvet paws and the cruel trap which is her mouth I smile. That industrious pink tongue, I say to myself, is but the preservation of the jungle instinct which warns her to remove all traces of her meal, so that she in turn shall not be tracked down for prey.

She understands my pleading and my anger, but acknowledges nothing. Serenely she goes her way. But when I do not want her she will come with me. Why should I love her?

Yet I will say that she is lovable. If she does not yield it is because she cannot. She is an exile among men, a monarch whose heritage must ever be preserved from decay and destruction. Without that heritage she must become man's servant, condemned forever to the scraps from his table.

Wise Amestris! A mistress who gives all is soon discarded. She who gives sparingly reigns forever.

Thus she tolerates me. In rare moments she fawns on me, deliciously surrendering her glossy warm body to my hands, singing throatily in ecstasy. Those amber eyes then penetrate my being, the exquisite grace of her melts my heart. She will play then, my Amestris, abandoning herself with laughter in her eyes to my foolish sport. But one false step and she will retreat to her cushioned throne, and see me not.

MESSALINA

Messalina is the solitary one, the lone huntress prowling through the long grass. Let the bird on the wing beware and the vole plunge to safety through the massed reeds, for Messalina is without mercy.

Her quivering body, silently coiled, springs more swiftly than the deadly arrow. Beneath her satin feet lurk sharp curved talons, strong as steel, and in the smooth, pink cavern of her mouth the white fangs await their prey.

In the shadows which cloak her coming and her going her jewelled eyes shine from their luminous depths. None can read their message, for Messalina is the solitary one. What restless, relentless spirit possesses this lean grey huntress?

She will not tarry with me nor be at rest, for as smoke drifts with the wind so must she vanish into the warm shadows. By the green depths of the forest stream she will crouch, silent and waiting, for the silver flash to stir her blood. The darting fish speeds on the surface of the water and is lost.

The lust of the hunter smoulders in her eyes, her silken limbs relax and with lashing tail she stretches on the crushed grass. The savoury morsel has appeased her hunger but soon she will hunger again.

In ambush she will wait, until the heat of the sun has passed and the cold moon gleams through the trellis of the green-black forest. Messalina is the solitary one.

ALACIEL

Scheming, arrogant and vain, the tawny queen demands obeisance. By crafty pride Alaciel has made me subject. Yet her royal demeanour is not counterfeit, for the blood of queens runs in her delicate veins, and pride is her rightful heritage.

I must needs pay tribute to her languid majesty. My voice is a caress, gentle and supplicating. The touch of my hand is as the courtier's bow, retreating at her queenly displeasure.

She is a tyrant, this Alaciel, and I am her devoted slave.

Vessels of the Orient, bring swiftly westward rare delicacies for her palate's delight! I cannot share with her my coarse meat and my sour bread.

Silken cushions will I strew for her, though straw be my bed. Cool shelter from the noonday sun shall be devised, lest clamour from the market-place disturb her rest.

Happy am I when she proudly accepts my favours. Lovely, tawny queen! Bowed down and humble am I when my offerings are despised. Cold, haughty mistress! Yet withal she is crafty for thus does she maintain her sovereignty.

My house is her palace and I tremble lest she forsake me. Her grace and beauty possess me utterly. She is a tyrant, this Alaciel, and I am her devoted slave.

THOMYRIS

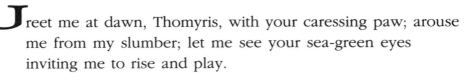

Greet me at dawn, Thomyris, with your caressing paw; arouse me from my slumber; let me see your sea-green eyes inviting me to rise and play.

Now morning is here, delicious and cool, and Thomyris beckons me from my couch. I rise and indolently stretch my limbs. She awaits me, motionless and grave. I speak to her; her eyes are on me but she does not answer. I am ready, Thomyris, let us play.

I move towards her; like a bronze statue gleaming in the sun's new rays she stands immovable. But lo! I reach for her and she has leapt away. That burnished flash escapes my outstretched hand and the sea-green eyes look down on me in gentle mockery.

Come, Thomyris, I will be kind. Softly will I clasp your supple form, softly will I whisper the flattery you love. Come, Thomyris, I am waiting.

You will not come to me? Then shall you pay the forfeit. Beware, Thomyris, for now you must be my captive. I will match your swiftness with my cunning. Twist and turn, it avails you not, for I cannot be denied. So. Now your are mine, Thomyris, and I will crush your soft warm body in my hands.

But no, I cannot. I must let you go. Who could resist the mute appeal of sea-green eyes? Enough of play; the sun is gathering strength and now to eat and drink together.

PASITHEA

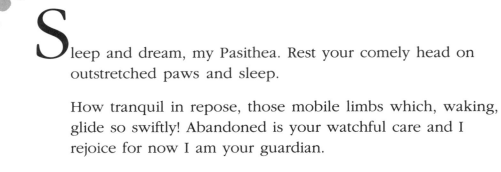

Sleep and dream, my Pasithea. Rest your comely head on outstretched paws and sleep.

How tranquil in repose, those mobile limbs which, waking, glide so swiftly! Abandoned is your watchful care and I rejoice for now I am your guardian.

You know, my Pasithea, you are safe with me. None shall disturb your slumber. Now is the time for rest. Dream of remembered pleasures and perchance, of me, whom now I think you love.

I will watch over you, Pasithea, even as I prepared your bed. They mock me, my foolish friends, but they do not understand. Why should I care for you as a mother for her babe? Why must I guard you?

Indeed you are a gentle creature and I love you for it. Your looks belie you, Pasithea, for the fiery ocelot whom you resemble is of strangely different temper.

Asleep, you are as beautiful in your frailty as the skirmishing butterfly, as timid as the coy gazelle. Who would suspect the strength that lies beneath the soft and tawny coat, the sharp perception of your eager eye?

Sleep, my Pasithea, and dream. Wake not yet, for while you lie relaxed and unaware I, too, may dream. For now I say you love me. When you wake my dream will likewise end, for well I know, my pretty, that you will stretch, and yawn, and stretch and yawn again.

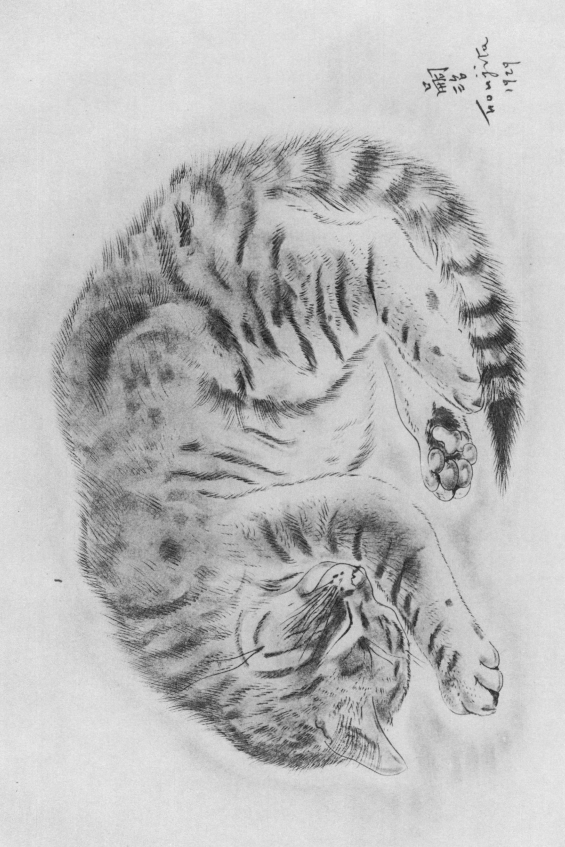

ERIGONE

Come to me, royal mistress, and let my hand caress your delicate, shapely head. I yearn to hear your throbbing song as I touch your silken fur. Let your slim beauty yield to my hand and invite again and yet again the soothing motion of my light caress.

For when your changing eyes look up at me and smile, exquisite is my delight. Why do you smile on me now? If I please you now why do I not please you always? Is not my caress the same?

Cannot you forget your royal birth? Must I always be the slave of your swift-changing mood, content in the radiance of your contentment, humble and penitent when you humble me?

Fool that I am to mar the happy moment by the thought of yesterday. Yet I know well that yesterday will come again tomorrow. So be it. The thought is spice, not poison. And your dominion could not be upheld if frowns did not sometimes usurp the place of favours.

So must I rejoice even as I am plaintive, knowing that the cause keeps love more vividly alive. Poor consolation! For I am tormented afresh by the mirage of your enduring love for me. When I am most sure of you you turn away.

Yet I will be content with what I have. So come to me, capricious, royal mistress, and let my hand caress you. Sing, delicately, turn voluptuously, gaze luminously into my eyes.